S0-AZD-500

The Declaration of Independence

by Rebecca Rissman

Content Consultant
William Pencak
Adjunct Professor of History
Ohio State University

CORE
LIBRARY

Published by ABDO Publishing Company, PO Box 398166, Minneapolis, MN 55439. Copyright © 2013 by Abdo Consulting Group, Inc. International copyrights reserved in all countries. No part of this book may be reproduced in any form without written permission from the publisher. The Core Library™ is a trademark and logo of ABDO Publishing Company.

Printed in the United States of America,
North Mankato, Minnesota
112012
012013
♻ THIS BOOK CONTAINS AT LEAST 10% RECYCLED MATERIALS.

Editor: Blythe Hurley
Series Designer: Becky Daum

Cataloging-in-Publication Data
Rissman, Rebecca.
 The Declaration of Independence / Rebecca Rissman.
   p. cm. -- (Foundations of our nation)
Includes bibliographical references and index.
ISBN 978-1-61783-758-6
1. United States. Declaration of Independence--Juvenile literature. 2. United States--Politics and government--1775-1783--Juvenile literature.   I. Title.
973.3/13--dc22

                                                    2012946538

Photo Credits: North Wind/North Wind Picture Archives, cover, 1, 6, 8, 15, 16, 22, 34, 36, 39; The Gainesville Sun/Matt Stamey/AP Images, 4; Hulton Archive/Getty Images, 12, 45; AP Images, 19, 25, 26, 33; DEA/M. Seemuller/Getty Images, 30; Red Line Editorial, 32; Hisham Ibrahim/Getty Images, 40

Cover: Continental Congress delegates sign the Declaration of Independence on July 4, 1776.

CONTENTS

CHAPTER ONE

The Roots of Rebellion

Americans celebrate Independence Day with fireworks, parades, and barbecues. But July 4 isn't just a day to have fun. It is also an important date in American history. It is when we celebrate the Declaration of Independence. This was the document that told the world the United States of America was a free country.

The Fourth of July is more than just a day for fireworks. We also celebrate the Declaration of Independence, the document that stated America was no longer a part of the British Empire.

George III was king of England leading up to and during the American Revolution.

Life in the Colonies

The United States did not exist in 1776. The people who would become Americans lived in 13 colonies. They were still ruled by King George III of Great Britain. The colonists had to follow British laws and pay taxes to Great Britain even though the king lived thousands of miles away.

Life was hard for many people living in the colonies. They faced difficult weather. They fought over land and resources with other Europeans and American Indians. The British government made life even harder for the colonists by making them pay new taxes. Many colonists felt this was unfair.

The British government passed the Stamp Act in 1765. This law forced colonists to buy special stamps to put on any printed papers. Newspapers could not be sold unless all the papers were stamped. Another new law called the Quartering Act was passed in 1765. It forced colonists to provide food and housing for British soldiers. Many colonists were unhappy with these laws.

The Tea Act was created in 1773. This law said only merchants who were loyal to Great Britain could sell British tea. Merchants who disagreed with British rules were in danger of losing their businesses. This attempt by Great Britain to control trade in America made colonists angrier.

On the night of December 16, 1773, a group of colonists in Boston, Massachusetts, boarded three British ships loaded with tea. The angry men threw

Colonists in New York City protest the Stamp Act in 1765.

342 chests of tea into the harbor in protest. This event became known as the Boston Tea Party.

The British government decided to stop the rebellion. A series of new rules gave the British more power than ever over life in the colonies. These laws closed Boston Harbor, among other harsh rules. The harbor would not reopen until the colonists paid for the tea they had destroyed.

People living in the colonies were divided into two groups. Some felt the colonies still needed British protection. Others argued the colonies should form a new country independent of Great Britain.

The First Continental Congress

All 13 colonies except Georgia sent representatives to a meeting called the First Continental Congress. It was held in Pennsylvania in 1774. It was not easy for the colonies to work together. They each had their own separate government and often fought with their neighbors about the colony borders.

Congress sent a message to King George III and the British government asking them to end their unpopular laws. The colonists said they would stop

The Sons of Liberty

A group of colonists who called themselves the Sons of Liberty began to gather in secret throughout the colonies. Another set of new laws called the Townshend Acts put more taxes in place in 1767. These laws taxed everyday items colonists imported from Great Britain. The Sons of Liberty wanted to protest these laws. They organized boycotts, or agreements not to buy British goods.

9

importing and exporting goods to and from Great Britain if the laws remained. King George III said no to the colonists' demands. He wanted the colonies to obey, even if it meant a war.

The Revolutionary War Begins

The colonists began to get ready for war with England. Colonists in Massachusetts collected guns and ammunition. They hid them in Concord. On their way to collect these weapons, British soldiers were interrupted by a group of colonists in Lexington. These men refused to let the soldiers march through their town without a fight. Both sides seemed ready for battle.

On April 19, 1775, a shot was fired. No one knows if it came from a British soldier or a colonist. The first battle had begun. The British defeated the colonists during the Battle of Lexington. But by the time the British reached Concord, most of the weapons were already gone. The colonists had hidden them. More colonists arrived to fight. They chased the British soldiers all the way back to Boston. Many

Timeline of Events Leading to the Battles of Lexington and Concord

This timeline shows the events that led up to the famous gunshot that marked the beginning of the Revolutionary War. What role did communication play in this event? How did the colonists' unusual forms of communication help them gain the upper hand against the British?

Date	Time	Event
April 18, 1775		Paul Revere warns the colonists of the British arrival.
April 19, 1775	12:30 a.m.	Revere's warning starts the colonists' warning system. Colonists signal fires and ring bells to alert other colonists to prepare to fight.
April 19, 1775	2:00 a.m.	British troops set out for Lexington.
April 19, 1775	Sunrise	The first shot is fired, and the Battle of Lexington begins. Eight colonists die, and nine are wounded. One British soldier is wounded.
April 19, 1775	7:00 a.m.	British troops arrive in Concord.
April 19, 1775	9:30 a.m.	British troops fire warning shots at the colonial militia. Colonists return fire and drive the British out all the way to Boston.

British soldiers were killed or wounded. This was the beginning of the Revolutionary War.

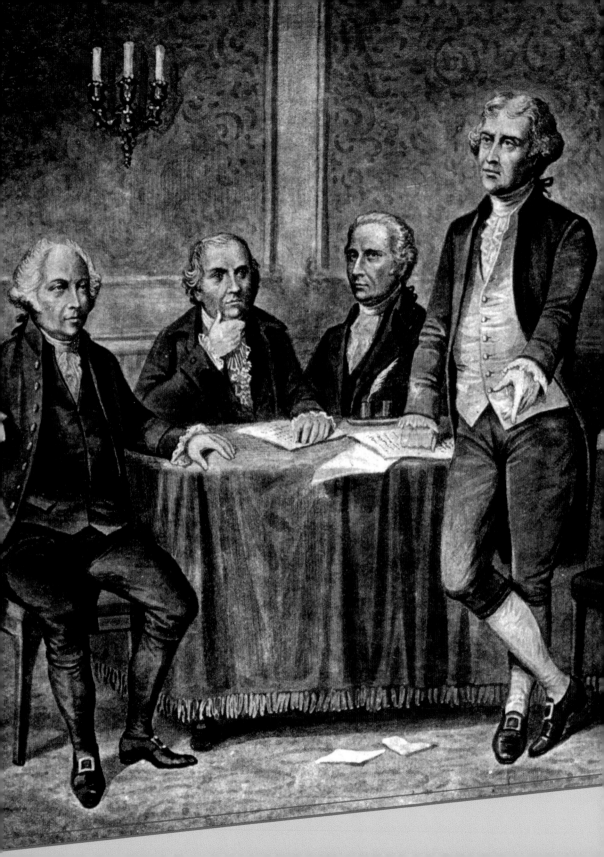

CHAPTER TWO

Turning to Independence

On May 10, 1775, representatives from all 13 colonies met for the Second Continental Congress. Some colonists still wanted to make peace with England. The Congress wrote a letter called the Olive Branch Petition to King George III. The letter asked him to stop the fighting until they could reach an agreement. The king refused. The colonists knew they had to fight.

John Adams, Robert Morris, Alexander Hamilton, and Thomas Jefferson at the Second Continental Congress, in 1775

The Battle of Bunker Hill

A large group of British soldiers arrived in Boston during June 1775. Colonial soldiers gathered on top of a hill in the nearby town of Charlestown to fight the British. British troops marched up the hill to battle on June 17. American soldier Colonel William Prescott told his soldiers to hold their fire until the British were very close. The British forces were badly hurt when the colonists did open fire. This became known as the Battle of Bunker Hill. The Americans eventually ran out of ammunition. Many were wounded or killed when the British finally captured the hill. But this battle sent an important message to the British troops. The colonists were strong and brave soldiers.

Shortly after the Battle of Bunker Hill, a tall, serious man from Virginia took control of the colonial soldiers. His name was George Washington. Washington was respected for the work he had done during the French and Indian War. Many colonists felt Washington would be a good military leader.

The Battle of Bunker Hill was one of the first major battles of the American Revolution.

Thomas Paine's *Common Sense*

In January 1776, a pamphlet called *Common Sense* was published. Many colonists read its message. It was written by a journalist named Thomas Paine. The pamphlet said the colonies should break away from Great Britain. It used simple reasons most colonists could understand. Paine did not like King George III

Captain William Prescott leads colonial soldiers during the Battle of Bunker Hill in 1775.

or any government ruled by kings or queens. He believed people should be able to choose their own rulers. He also said America could be an independent country with a new government. More than 500,000 copies of *Common Sense* were sold within a few months.

The Lee Resolution

During the spring of 1776, more colonists were ready to break free from Great Britain. A Virginia man named Richard Henry Lee brought a resolution to Congress on June 7. The Lee Resolution bravely called the colonies independent states. This meant continued fighting between British and colonial soldiers would not be a civil war fought between people of the same country. This was a war between England and the American states.

Congress talked about Lee's ideas. Some members were still unsure. Declaring independence might hurt relationships with British merchants. The colonists would lose British protection from other countries. The colonists had to worry about their own safety. Benjamin Franklin wrote that the colonists must stick together or there would be consequences. Franklin was telling the colonists their actions were dangerous. It was important to stand united against Great Britain.

"I Am Obnoxious, Suspected, and Unpopular"

The Committee of Five argued over who should write the Declaration of Independence. Adams thought Jefferson should be the author. When Jefferson disagreed, Adams told him, "Reason first, you are a Virginian, and a Virginian ought to appear at the head of this business. Reason second, I am obnoxious, suspected, and unpopular. You are very much otherwise. Reason third, you can write ten times better than I can." Jefferson agreed to do his best.

The Committee of Five

On June 11, 1776, five men were named to write a declaration of independence. The group was called the Committee of Five. It included Benjamin Franklin, John Adams, Roger Sherman, Robert Livingston, and Thomas Jefferson.

Jefferson was chosen to be the Declaration's main author. He finished a rough draft and brought it to the other men in the committee. Together they revised the draft. Jefferson then presented it to Congress on June 28, 1776. He called it

John Adams considered himself too "obnoxious, suspected, and unpopular" to serve as the main author of the Declaration of Independence.

FURTHER EVIDENCE

New British taxes and laws angered the American colonists. This pushed them closer to war with Great Britain. Review Chapter Two. Identify its main point. Try to find three examples of supporting evidence. Then go to the Web site below to read the lyrics of a song sung by British supporters during the war. Do the song's words support the main point of this chapter? Or do they present another point of view?

The Rebels
www.digitalhistory.uh.edu/learning_history/revolution/rebels.cfm

"A Declaration by the Representatives of the United States Of America in General Congress Assembled." This was the document that would become the Declaration of Independence.

Thomas Paine's pamphlet *Common Sense* was written in a simple way for an audience of common people. This work convinced many colonists it was time to fight for independence:

As to government matters, it is not in the power of Britain to do this continent justice. . . . The business of it will soon be too weighty, and intricate, to be managed with any tolerable degree of convenience, by a power, so distant from us, and so very ignorant of us . . . for if they cannot conquer us, they cannot govern us. To be always running three or four thousand miles with a tale or a petition, waiting four or five months for an answer, which when obtained requires five or six more to explain it in, will in a few years be looked upon as folly and childishness. . . . There was a time when it was proper, and there is a proper time for it to cease.

Source: Thomas Paine. Common Sense. 1776. Archiving Early America. Archiving Early America, 2012. Web. Accessed November 9, 2012.

What's the Big Idea?

Thomas Paine made many arguments about why the American colonies should be free from British rule. What is the main point he is making here? How does he support his point? Try to find two supporting details.

CHAPTER THREE

Inside the Declaration of Independence

Jefferson was chosen to write the Declaration of Independence because he was an excellent writer. He had published an essay in 1774. In it he made bold statements about British rule. Many colonists found this essay shocking. They also found it well written and convincing. Jefferson had written it without signing his name. But many people knew he was the author. Jefferson also wrote a draft of

The Continental Congress met in Philadelphia, Pennsylvania's, Independence Hall to write the Declaration of Independence in 1776.

a proposed constitution for Virginia. Jefferson was a smart author. The other representatives felt he could handle the important job of putting a nation's thoughts on paper.

The Five Parts

Jefferson wrote the Declaration of Independence in five parts. They were an introduction, a preamble, a list of complaints about the leadership of King George III, a list of complaints about the British people, and a conclusion.

The Introduction says the colonists found it necessary to get rid of any political connections with Great Britain. Jefferson's choice of the word *necessary* told readers the colonists had thought carefully about their actions. They were not asking for permission to become a new country. They were taking action.

The Preamble explains the beliefs and ideals of the new American government. It says all men are created equal and have rights that cannot be taken

Jefferson in 1786

away. It points to the rights to life, liberty, and the pursuit of happiness. It notes it is a government's duty to protect these rights. Finally, it explains governments that do not protect these rights should be removed from power. The Preamble does not

One important section of the Declaration listed the colonists' complaints against King George III.

mention the British government or the American people. Instead, it uses general language that could be applied to any people.

The third section lists 27 separate offenses, or unfair actions, King George III carried out against the colonists. It accuses King George III of going to war with the colonists, not letting them make their own laws, and cutting off their trade with the rest of the world.

The fourth section lists the offenses of the British people against the colonists. It was not enough to point out King George III's unfair actions. The Declaration also said the British people had not protected the colonists. It explains the colonists had warned the British citizens that British rule was unfair. It claims the British had ignored them. This paragraph makes it clear the colonists no longer felt connected to the British people.

King George's Offenses

The list of King George's offenses is usually divided into four groups:

- The king's abuse of power over colonial governments. This included keeping an army during peacetime.
- The king's unfair actions against the colonists. This included taking away their ability to trade with other countries.
- The king's violent actions against the colonies. These included declaring war and killing colonists.
- Every request by the colonists for help or protection had been met with the king's cruelty.

The Conclusion of the Declaration states the colonies are now free and independent states. It says the United States may make war, establish peace, form relationships and trade with other countries, and act in all ways as a free and independent country.

Signing this document was dangerous. Every person who signed it could have been charged with treason against Great Britain.

EXPLORE ONLINE

Jefferson wrote in the Declaration of Independence that "all men are created equal." Yet Jefferson himself was a slave owner. In fact, many of the men involved in the American Revolution owned slaves or supported slavery. Visit the Web site below to explore the role of slavery in the American colonies. Compare the information you find there with the ideas set out in the Declaration of Independence. Are they different? How?

Jefferson and Slavery at Monticello
www.monticello.org/slavery-at-monticello

The Declaration of Independence explained the rights the Founding Fathers believed all men should have. Read an excerpt below:

> *We hold these truths to be self-evident, that all men are created equal, that they are endowed by their Creator with certain unalienable Rights, that among these are Life, Liberty and the pursuit of Happiness. . . . That to secure these rights, Governments are instituted among Men, deriving their just powers from the consent of the governed. . . . That whenever any Form of Government becomes destructive of these ends, it is the Right of the People to alter or to abolish it, and to institute new Government, laying its foundation on such principles and organizing its powers in such form, as to them shall seem most likely to effect their Safety and Happiness.*
>
> *Source: Thomas Jefferson. "The Declaration of Independence." 1776. The Charters of Freedom. US National Archives, n.d. Web. Accessed November 9, 2012.*

Consider Your Audience

Review this passage. Consider how you would adapt it for a different audience, such as your parents or friends. Write a blog post conveying this same information for the new audience. Write it so it can be understood by them. What is the most effective way to get your point across? How does your new approach differ from the original text, and why?

CHAPTER FOUR

Signing the Declaration

The Lee Resolution said all political connection between the colonies and Great Britain would be gone. While Jefferson and the rest of the committee were busy working on the Declaration, Congress had not yet decided whether the colonies should become independent. Congress did not decide until July 2. Twelve colonies voted to approve the Lee Resolution on July 2.

Colonists pull down a statue of King George III in New York City to celebrate American Independence in July 1776.

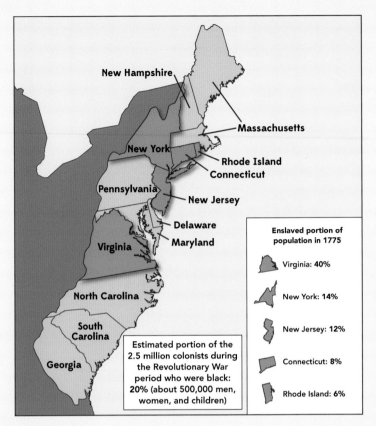

The map shows the 13 colonies: New Hampshire, Massachusetts, New York, Rhode Island, Connecticut, Pennsylvania, New Jersey, Delaware, Maryland, Virginia, North Carolina, South Carolina, Georgia.

Enslaved portion of population in 1775

Virginia: 40%

New York: 14%

New Jersey: 12%

Connecticut: 8%

Rhode Island: 6%

Estimated portion of the 2.5 million colonists during the Revolutionary War period who were black: 20% (about 500,000 men, women, and children)

Slavery in Colonial America

Few colonists kept slaves when the colonies were first created. But slavery was present in all 13 colonies by 1776. This graphic shows the number of slaves living in the colonies when the Declaration was written. What does this tell you about the colonists' attitudes toward slavery? How do you think colonists would have reacted if Jefferson's criticism of slavery had been left in the Declaration?

Now Congress was certain the colonies should become an independent nation. But they needed to make sure the Declaration of Independence explained the feelings of the new country perfectly.

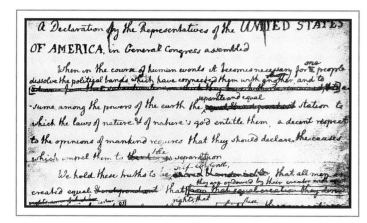

An original rough draft of the Declaration showing the editing marks of its authors

From July 2 to July 4, Congress talked about the Declaration. Congress only made one large change to the document. They took out Jefferson's statements about England's role in the slave trade. Many colonists depended on slaves in their everyday lives at that time. Congress was not ready to make this difficult issue a part of the Declaration.

Once Congress was happy with their changes, they voted to approve the Declaration of Independence on July 4, 1776. The president of Congress, John Hancock, and Charles Thomson, its secretary, signed the document. Congress then ordered the Committee of Five to make copies of the Declaration and send them to leaders throughout the

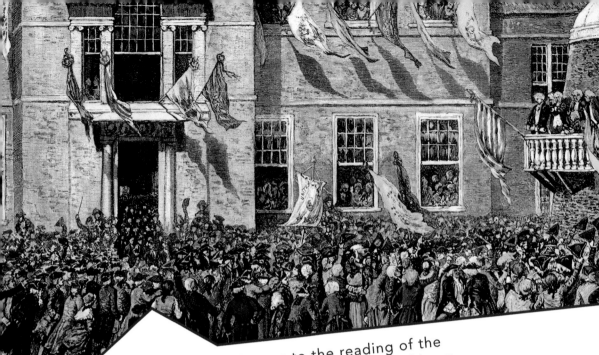

An excited crowd listens to the reading of the Declaration of Independence in Philadelphia on July 4, 1776.

colonies. It was important for all Americans to know their government had declared independence from Great Britain. They were no longer living in British colonies. They were living in the United States.

On July 9, the Declaration was read aloud to Washington and his troops in New York. A crowd of excited Americans pulled down a statue of King George III in a park in New York City. This statue was eventually melted to make bullets for the Americans to use against the British.

Congress Signs the Declaration

On July 19, Congress directed the Declaration be signed by every member of Congress. Most of the representatives gathered to sign the final copy on August 2. Hancock was again the first to sign. The rest of the Congress members placed their signatures based on the locations of their states. New Hampshire, the most northern state, began the list of signatures at the top right side. Georgia, the state farthest to the south, ended the list at the left side.

Too Soon to Sign?

Not everyone who voted to approve the Declaration of Independence on July 4 actually signed it. John Dickinson did not sign because he was still hopeful for peace between the colonies and Great Britain. Even Robert Livingston, a member of the Committee of Five, decided not to sign the document. He thought it was too soon for the colonies to become an independent country.

CHAPTER FIVE

What Does the Declaration Mean to Us?

By the end of the summer of 1776, the Declaration of Independence had been sent to leaders throughout the states. The Americans were not able to celebrate for long. They were still fighting a brutal war against the British. The Americans needed help fighting the large and powerful British army.

The British army surrenders to George Washington in 1781.

In 1778 the French and American governments reached an agreement to work together against Great Britain. Spain also joined the war against Great Britain in 1779. The Americans were able to beat the British with the help of the French and the Spanish. The war was over! Three American representatives traveled to Paris, France, where the Treaty of Paris was signed in 1783. This document officially ended the Revolutionary War. It also said Great Britain accepted the independence of the United States.

The Declaration of Independence and the Constitution

The Declaration of Independence said the United States of America was a new country. But the Declaration did not create a government for the citizens of the United States. The new government was created by the United States Constitution in 1787. This document had to be agreed on by voters in all 13 states.

American and French representatives sign a treaty during the American Revolution. French military assistance was essential to American victory in the war.

The preamble of the Declaration says a government should get its power from the people it governs. The Constitution also says it is written by the people. This meant the people of a country should agree to the rules of its government.

Visiting the Declaration of Independence

Today you can see the Declaration of Independence at the National Archives in Washington DC. The ink is badly faded because the document was not well

The original Declaration of Independence is on display at the National Archives in Washington DC.

preserved during the 1800s. It is now kept under protective glass in a special case for safety.

A Symbol of American Freedom

The Declaration of Independence is a symbol of American freedom and ideals. It represents the colonists' break from the unfair and cruel British government. It also represents the bravery of the colonists. They risked their lives to form a better government.

Each year on July 4, we celebrate the actions of the colonists. We remember their bravery and their commitment to freedom. When we light fireworks or watch parades on Independence Day, we are celebrating the Declaration of Independence and the creation of the United States of America.

No National Treasure Map

The feature film *National Treasure* told a story about a secret map printed in invisible ink on the back of the Declaration of Independence. Some people still think there is a map or secret words on the back of the Declaration. But all it actually says is "Original Declaration of Independence, dated July 4, 1776." The document was probably kept rolled up at one time. This note was an easy way for people to know what the document was without having to open it.

IMPORTANT DATES

1765

The Stamp Act is ordered into effect by King George III. The Quartering Act is passed by Parliament.

1767

The Townshend Acts create new taxes on everyday goods the colonists import from Great Britain.

1773

The Boston Tea Party takes place in Boston, Massachusetts, on December 16.

1775

The Battle of Bunker Hill takes place in Charlestown, Massachusetts, on June 17.

1775

George Washington takes command of the Continental Army.

1776

The Committee of Five is appointed to write the Declaration of Independence on June 11.

42

1774

The first Continental Congress takes place in Philadelphia.

1775

A shot is fired in Lexington, Massachusetts, on April 19.

1775

The Second Continental Congress begins in Philadelphia on May 10.

1776

The Declaration of Independence is drafted and debated by the Committee of Five and Congress during June and July.

1776

Congress adopts the Declaration of Independence on July 4. The first copies are printed.

1776

The Declaration of Independence is signed by almost all members of Congress on August 2.

Why Do I Care?

Are there any parallels between the story of the Declaration of Independence and your own life? Have you ever had to debate with friends or loved ones about the right thing to do in a difficult situation? Have you ever had to take a risk to accomplish something that was important to your family or community? Have you ever felt that one of your rights was being taken away unjustly?

You Are There

Imagine you are a colonist living in Boston, Massachusetts, in the time leading up to the Revolutionary War. Write 300 words describing your life. What do you see happening in your town? Are there any protests? How do you feel about the British government? You may wish to look up information about the Boston Massacre and the Boston Tea Party in order to help you tell this story.

Surprise Me

Think about what you learned about the writing of the Declaration of Independence. Can you name the two or three facts in this book that you found most surprising? Write a short paragraph about each, describing what you found surprising and why.

Tell the Tale

This book discusses how the Stamp Act affected the colonists. Write 200 words that tell the true story of how the Stamp Act was received in the colonies. Be sure to set the scene, develop a sequence of events, and offer a conclusion.

GLOSSARY

colony
a community settled in a new area that is governed by a parent country

constitution
a document establishing the form and powers of a government

draft
a rough version of a piece of writing from which a final version may be produced

export
to sell goods to another country

import
to buy goods from another country

Parliament
the national governing body of Great Britain

preamble
a special introduction to a larger statement or piece of writing

rebellion
the act of fighting or resisting a power

representatives
members of a government who stand for a group of people

resolution
a statement of a governing body's opinion

tax
money paid to a governing body

treason
criminal actions against a ruling government

LEARN MORE

Books

Aronson, Marc. *The Real Revolution: The Global Story of American Independence.* New York: Clarion Books, 2005.

Murphy, Daniel P. *The Everything American Revolution Book.* Avon, MA: Adams Media, 2008.

Pierce, Alan. *The Declaration of Independence.* Edina, MN: ABDO, 2005.

Web Links

To learn more about the Declaration of Independence, visit ABDO Publishing Company online at **www.abdopublishing.com**. Web sites about the Declaration are featured on our Book Links page. These links are routinely monitored and updated to provide the most current information available.

Visit **www.mycorelibrary.com** for free additional tools for teachers and students.

INDEX

ABOUT THE AUTHOR

Rebecca Rissman is an award-winning author and editor of children's nonfiction. She has written more than 100 books about history, science, and art. She lives in Portland, Oregon, with her husband and enjoys hiking, yoga, and cooking.